ALONE IN CHURCH

Saint Julian Press

Poetry

PRAISE for ALONE IN CHURCH

This powerful and poignant collection, which explores themes as diverse as the experiences of those marginalized by autism, or by the neglect of feminine spirituality, we find a universal appeal in the most homely and holy, modest and grand, resistant and healing of moments. Each line is inevitable, the craftsmanship—like the poet's vision—full of grace and light. I welcomed the world of the poems entirely, thankful for being allowed to share in the speaker's remarkable experience.

Carol Guerrero-Murphy, Professor Emerita, author of
Table Walking at Nighthawk (2007) and *Chained Dog Dreams* (2019).

Dr. Messineo's personal witness and poetic work on Asperger's and spirituality is a rich and varied study.

J.Pittman McGehee, D.D., Episcopal Priest
and Diplomate Jungian Analyst, author of
The Invisible Church (2009) and *Growing Down* (2013).

I wept after reading the manuscript. Andrea compassionately and sensitively addresses both the spiritual longing and hunger, and the difficulties navigating that need with the need for solitude. Andrea's work creates a space for people with Asperger's to explore their spiritual yearning.

D. Scott Stanley, Ph.D.
Psychotherapist, Houston TX

ALONE IN CHURCH

Poems

by

Andrea Messineo

SAINT JULIAN PRESS
HOUSTON

Published by
SAINT JULIAN PRESS, Inc.
2053 Cortlandt, Suite 200
Houston, Texas 77008

www.saintjulianpress.com

Copyright © 2019
Two Thousand and Nineteen
© Andrea Messineo

ISBN-13: 978-1-7320542-9-5
ISBN: 1-7320542-9-0
Library of Congress Control Number: 2019941141

Cover Art: *Abbey of Sant'Antimo* by Ron Starbuck
Author Photo by Danielle Chisler

❖

PREFACE

❖

My impression of poetry from high school literature was one of intentionally obscured images, creating a coded language that I was meant to tease out at great length. Midway through life's journey, I spent years trying to write down my experiences of Church, but struggled to find the right form. Much as I aspired to a sweeping historical genre, my own efforts in that direction never came together. Something in the nature of the sacred eluded my grasp, and resisted my efforts to write in such an affirmative manner.

With the encouragement of several friends and guides, I allowed interior practices, like centering prayer and dreamwork, to influence my writing. These practices help us to gently set aside the voice of the ego, to access inner sources of symbol, meaning, and connectedness. Not far along this path, I began to describe spiritual experience in a language appropriate to its mystery. To no one's surprise more than my own, that language is poetry!

Many of these poems deal with themes of misunderstanding and alienation, especially on the part of those coping with physical or neurological difference. Reflection on the interconnected framework of spectrum traits – both strengths and challenges – has helped me to make sense of my journey, and also of the historical witness given by certain extraordinary people of faith. It may be that some autistic-seeming traits are hard to distinguish from attributes of persons who feel not-at-home between the seen and unseen worlds.

Andrea Messineo
Houston, August 2019

FOR JERRY RUHL,
WHO SAW THE POETRY IN MY PROSE.

CONTENTS

THE BEGINNING OF LABOR	1
ART	2
SPRING FLOWERS	3
ANOTHER	4
PILGRIMAGE	5
CHRISTMAS EVE	6
DEATH OF LILACS	7
BREAD AND WINE	8
ICON GALLERY	9
SILENCE	10
MID-DAY EXAM	11
MIGRAINE	12
BRIDGING THE GAP	14
ALL-NIGHT DINER	15
SCRUPULOSITY	16
AFTERNOONS ON AVENTINE HILL	17
THE STREETS OF ROME	18
LOGOS IN THREE MOVEMENTS	19
POP PSYCHOLOGY	20
GOSSIP	21
PARABLE OF THE TALENTS	22
DARK MOTHER	23
O ANTIPHONS	24
WATER CREATURES	26
CHRIST-BEARER	27
EUCHARISTIC ADORATION	28
BEHAVIORAL HOSPITAL	29
LOST FRIEND	30
HOPE	31
LEONIE MARTIN	32
POOR MAN, RICH MAN	33
STEALING AWAY	34
AGNES OF MONTPULCIANO	35
HEDDLES	36
SACRED HEART	37
ARM'S LENGTH	38
THE LAST DAY	39
AGING PRAYER	40
GLIMPSING NEW MEXICO	41
CAT	42

One day (Francis) went out into the countryside to meditate. Finding himself passing by the church of San Damiano, which threatened to fall down – old as it was – and driven by the impulse of the Holy Spirit, he went inside to pray. Kneeling in prayer before the image of the Crucified,… he heard with his bodily ears a voice come down to him from the cross and say to him three times: "Francis, go and rebuild my church which, as you see, is all in ruins!" Upon hearing that voice, Francis was amazed and trembling, because he was alone in church.

- St. Bonaventure, *Leggenda Maggiore (Life of St. Francis)* II, 1038. Translation – Andrea Messineo.

ALONE IN CHURCH

THE BEGINNING OF LABOR

In the stillness and anticipation
of an Annunciation,
she inclines her head like a queen
and consents to be born.

ART

Peeling every carrot into ribbons
without rushing, sensing their loveliness

Sweeping the floors carefully
while we inwardly sit at high councils

As we once lingered over our paper
and deliberated the just choice of color.

We lost ourselves for hours
lovingly tracing the outlines of each leaf.

Self-propelled wheels,
playing before God like daughter Wisdom.

We had no need to be *patient*,
there where there is no time.

We used to know how to re-enter eternity
when we were young.

SPRING FLOWERS

Forsythia – little yellow trumpets on russet canes,
the first to herald spring's approach after frosts.

Hyacinth – thick perfume wafting from a cascade of bells,
improbably wedged between stone wall and yard.

Clumps of buttery daffodils, standing at attention,
amidst grassy leaves that were bent by sudden winds.

Crocus – rare secret, ultraviolet around a radiant stamen sun,
to be found behind only certain silvery birches.

Thinking I discovered all these alone, I hunted them carefully,
forgetting my own parents must have first shown them to me

and indeed conveyed delight in the game of searching for them,
having thought to make a home in a place where flowers grew.

So too, when we think we have found some spiritual insight
by our own efforts, does Our Father let us joy in the discovery.

Though it was Love that came before, and also prepared the way,
Love lets itself be thus forgotten, and rediscovered in a flower.

ANOTHER

How astonishing to find,
in the faded pages of history,
One who stood, living, and
fixed me with a gaze of love!

No less than if walking
through a gallery of marble statues
with blush and linen rustle
One bowed and took my hand.

Words are not needed;
for such companionship
changes little, changes all,
and his eyes are not forgotten.

They allow me sometimes
to see, accompany another.
Changes little, but the gift is
the seed of all change.

PILGRIMAGE

We would walk hip-deep through snow
black dog arcing over like a seal
sun catching a glassy net of iced brambles
and dazzling them into cathedral glory.
Piping cardinals and chickadees
would flit from tree to tree,
following in our train
as we trudged the quarter-mile or so
down the country lane
on a pilgrimage to the mailbox.
Few young people would understand now
(when news flows over and around us):
Why undertake such an arduous journey
just to get news of the outside world?
Why leave the warm comfort of home
on the chance that – among the bills –
would be tucked a seed catalog,
holding dreams for spring, or even
a handwritten letter from a friend?
Those were the last days, perhaps
in which it was possible
to grow up solitary.

CHRISTMAS EVE

Crowded around a single heating vent
in the floor of the dark, frigid church
so that the warmed air will find its way inside
their hand-me-down winter coats and skirts,
the girls sing carols in the choir.

Faithful remnant gathered –
not in the luxuriously carpeted
and glassed-in complex up the road,
where well-maintained cars whisk worshippers away
having barely felt the chill between vestibule and cabin,

but in the pilgrim church away
across frozen, windswept fields
too poor to afford much more than candlelight
and no reason to remove any layer of woolen wrapping
while midnight Mass proceeds.

As the grizzled old priest
gets into his doughty black Oldsmobile
to travel through the holy night
(for he is expected at sunrise in another state)
he praises the hopeful choir, "You did a really fine job."

DEATH OF LILACS

Stately, abundant lilac tree
tossing its branches
pillowed with pale lavender blooms
that perfume the air
ahead of sudden summer storms.

Time yet before we have to go in.
A child plays on the patio
where the adults visit over iced tea,
and debate over dogma.
A wife coughs and smiles politely.

Wind rising, clouds scudding, petals swirling.
The host becomes more insistent:
"So was the blood spilled for all or for many?"
In retreat, the guests demur, the women
saying good-bye over battle-lines
for the final time in a long friendship.

Sudden hoofbeats – four goats out of their
enclosure, stripping the tender lilac bark.
Child staring open-mouthed,
parents yelling and chasing,
then tending to the tree's hurts. If only
the bark had not been peeled all around...

BREAD AND WINE

Crackle of slow-baked crust
springy threads of crumb,
resisting delightfully before
giving way to pillowy white softness.

Dusky elegance of grapes
wonderfully mouth-sized.
Smooth skin, pops at a bite,
their luscious purple-red juice dribbling.

These ancient comforts overinvolve me
who did not have to fight –
at least – for them;
I use them as a stay, a refuge.

Turned clumsy and inward,
I cannot take then let go easily
but must rely on rubrics
to stand between me and pleasure.

Yet a little portion taken and shared
placed not in my own mouth first
throws me beyond sense, and
closes the round of fellowship.

ICON GALLERY

For some, their truest self
flows into being word by word
from pen or keyboard; but evanesces
whenever mouth is opened to speak.

And for some, the selves that they write
ought not (they've learned) be spoken;
and so in digital anonimity they try on
various exertions and characters.

In each of us, the self is a longer story
than ever we have begun to tell; and
the selves are multivalent, more so
than the sides in any online debate.

The icon painters of old, monks and nuns,
were said to "write" their holy pictures,
since they did so not for pleasurable gaze
but to give instruction in the symbols.

And so we write our several lives like icons.
We speak with them, to better learn to speak.
They answer us through symbols unexpected:
a multitude of sacred patrons there to guide.

SILENCE

He dreamed he beat upon a glass wall
but no one heard on the other side.
Then, as all spoke easily in a round
he broke through at an inopportune time.

They grasped for his hands and face
and asked for his credentials
under harsh glare and echoing din
in pressing crowds inescapable.

Then waking, he sees to his right and
to his left, clothed in snowdrift attire,
brothers standing in solemn joy
bearing witness to their love in silence.

By the welcome of that soundless word,
detours and exclusions are repaired;
Alpha and Omega points come together,
the harm of Babel is undone.

MID-DAY EXAM

At the noon hour
before assembling to eat
the monastics examine their conscience
to see in what way they may have offended.

Before the sun runs its course
they pause to gather up what was hasty,
overlooked – not what was done to them
but, in the mystical way of things, their
own part – to make amends.

How hard it is to hold at the mid-point
between one heated action and the next
and to see unlove infiltrating like darkness:
radical courage.

And how gracious the curiosity
of a brother or sister who thinks
perhaps I misunderstood,
or speak a different language,
"Excuse me."

MIGRAINE

The faultline between the hemispheres,
between the East of glorious ruins
and the West of stinking refineries,
slipped out of my mind and into my body
where it split my head in two.

Glimpses retained in memory
of blindingly reflected sunlight
make the whole scene *de trop*, too much.
Like a photograph that is overexposed,
the excesses of light and heat bring with them a darker side:

Constant dampness, creeping mold, filthy roaches
in the recesses of every house; and predictably,
as the storm clouds roll in from the Gulf every few days:
retreat into darkened rooms with the no-action,
no-speech, no-thought of migraine.

No mere stab or ache – that indeed could well be ignored.
Instead, it is an unease in the whole of one's being,
as when on board ship in a rolling sea.
A shift to uncanny perceptions, as when yellow and purple
thunderheads cast shadows over the summer landscape.

It is a sense of panic and violation
to know the intruder is there with you
in the safe room of your own head.

In the time before, when the aura gives its warning,
there is a busyness together with rituals of warding.
We take rescue medications, and ask "Will they work?"
"Did I wait too long?"
We do all the other things that may have stopped
the night flower from blooming in the past.

Store up provisions, make arrangements while we still can,
for the hours when we will be immobile, like Christ on the Cross.
When the migraine is upon me, I would wish to pray
but can only briefly glimpse a prior intention, as the lament
"My God, my God, why have you forsaken me?" intones
a cherished psalm then fades away.

There is a need to find an equilibrium or poise inside of the
nothingness,
 to take up a stance outside of one's self
from which the pain can be observed,
rather than frantically seeking to escape it.
The path of flight leads nowhere profitable.

If I am able, I sometimes seek consolation in places of worship,
only to be met with glaring lights, reverberating mics,
people joyfully shouting.
Is there nowhere to be found what used to be called a "low Mass,"
with quiet recitation of the service by candlelight?

BRIDGING THE GAP

Heart thudding in his throat,
palms sweating as he clutched
driving directions to fellowship:
they were taking the Beltway.

In his mind the elevated overpass
morphed into spiraling cloverleafs
impossibly high and complex;
but he knew no other way.

His eyes flicker toward the leader
used to shepherding large numbers
toward activities of goodness,
who has no returning glance.

Shamefaced, he asks the kind girl
for a ride, murmuring some excuse.
After a half-beat's hesitation,
caught off guard, she agrees.

Entering the Beltway together,
impossibly high and complex,
he looks over and sees her
fingers white-knuckled on the wheel.

ALL-NIGHT DINER

At the entrance to the church
a scold blocked my path, hands on hips,
with her two ill-mannered children.

Scarcely had I got around them
when I started looking for a seat,
following choir stalls around the back
as they spiraled outward like a seashell.

And each person, alone in a booth,
lost themselves listening to podcasts,
surfed, or otherwise did as they liked.

As the seats curved gently around,
they opened into fragrant tables
where people faced one another
and were nourished at all hours.

I found a place together with some I knew.
The man across from me asked my opinion;
I said we'd not yet seen each other's potential.

SCRUPULOSITY

A slowing down of thought, of will.
Was this well done? Was that left undone?
A seizing of gears as from ice congealing
where others tread easily through meadows.

Our every creeping movement is halted
and searched with the floodlight of mind
to pin the unruly urges, dangerous instincts
that skitter for cover, always one blink ahead.

Then nothing for it but to atone anew;
yet our tired brain loses the count – was it today,
or yesterday the fault was done? Our proud heart
adds, was it fault at all, or did we never decide?

To our friends we are become as carved in marble.
We think it is a small price for salvation,
yet we cannot come to the end of the arguments:
the voice of the Accuser drones ever on.

Until we may meet the pitying eyes of One
who stands by, and take his hand for the dance.
What have I to do with safety? he asks;
I am not safe.

AFTERNOONS ON AVENTINE HILL

We study, desultory, the ontological argument
poring over massive tomes in the library of St. Anselm's
as motes spiral between the carrells until – good intentions defeated
– we put notes away, to read in a cramped room at night.

For the sun is out, and we students stride laughing
to flop down amidst the roses and eat our crusty bread and ham
and talk loudly in our various languages, heedless of the slowly
perambulating Italians, who wear woolen overcoats in May.

Walk back up the hill: if it is an off hour for tourists, we peek
into the cartoon keyhole without waiting in line, see St. Peter's dome.
Duck into St. Alexius for some shade; when eyes adjust, view the story
of the saint who lived as a beggar under the steps of his father's house.

Take the paths among the orange groves, sweet fragrance in the air.
Careless of pleasure, we take for granted frothy blooms twice in a year,
as we look out over the city – expanses of marble rose-pink in the dusk
– and forget to consider why we never see fruit.

Solemn Mass in St. Sabina's; people crowd in to see the Pope
except for a large bare circle around a kneeling, fresh-faced girl.
One of Mother Teresa's nuns, who has been washing the homeless'
clothes all day, and her white and blue habit stinks to high heaven.

THE STREETS OF ROME

Suffocating exhaust
of the roaring buses that everywhere disgorge
their passengers: stout housewives with pullcarts
on their way to open-air fruit and vegetable markets;
rushed business men who side-step, cursing,
tourists conferring and consulting maps
who – together with the priests and nuns –
swell to five million a city built to hold only one.
Forced by the crowd into a puddle, you squelch on a
wet shoe for hours. Espresso machines hiss
in cafés on every corner. Hungry as you may be,
you can scarcely walk in public eating, any more
than the ancient Romans could and not be judged uncouth.
Keep walking, carrying your heavy bag through the alleys,
until you pass the grimy door to some moribund parish.
Duck inside, and lo! A dazzling fresco soars overhead,
sunlight streams through the cupola, covered in cherubim.
In an alcove, an incorrupt saint patiently waits,
arms crossed, his soul's return on the Last Day.

LOGOS IN THREE MOVEMENTS

It seemed at one time that the message I should write
would spring forth entire like the facets of a jewel

each part connected to the next as with a running fire
giving off both light and heat against the darkness.

And if I hurried I could transcribe it all down
before the vouchsafed image faded away.

At another time I shot up into the realm of ideas
and covered myself with them as with clouds.

I wielded them like hail or thunderbolts
with nothing to dull their edge but a wry smile.

But then came a warmth, a thawing, and I fell back down
into a plodding world where I could no longer duel.

As by a half-remembered craft, I placed one word before the other
then looked again to see what those together had made.

And then, having forgotten the words, in horror of the game,
I prayed to know where the bright images had gone.

After a long time, deep underwater, I began to sense
them bodied forth in all that is, thanks to His Body.

One need not see at all to work, it seems; I go
as a blind craftsman, by touch, in the dark.

POP PSYCHOLOGY

"Only you can find the answers within."
Another abandonment.
Why speak as if to one dispersed, needing to be invited in?

When she is more like the woman in the Gospels,
who lit a lamp
and swept the whole house, to find her lost coin?

If she has called in a neighbor for help,
be sure she has looked everywhere
and the coin is not there.

Tell her that the house has a basement.

GOSSIP

The brisk Italian housemaid, apron pinned on in front,
hands a towel and bucket to the American student
and gestures toward the floors.

But the woman receives in reply merely a bemused smile
that she and her friends will later interpret to mean
"Surely you don't intend for me to wash them?"
(The student was waiting for some kind of handle
to affix to the cloth – every mop has one, no?)

The talk drew new vigor around how very *angrily*
the student banged the dishes together after drying them.
(Heavy, glazed ceramic, threatening every moment
to slip out of the linen towels and shatter on the tiles –
so different from the light dinnerware
she had been used to rinse and set in a draining rack.)

Matters came to a head
as she left the house before dawn day after day
eschewing morning Eucharist with the community –
a household of sisters who never went anywhere,
and so had no concept of rush hour, or university chapels.

After a few months of this,
the head of the boarding house calls to the student on the stairs,
says, "you know you cannot come back next year."
And since there was with her a great dearth of words
to match the words that were said all-unknown about her,
as silently as she had stayed, she goes.

PARABLE OF THE TALENTS

The preacher interrupts our comfortable thoughts
of preparation for the holidays,
speaking strenuously as if from great conviction:
"Do not neglect the talents the Lord has given you!"

Heads of families shift uncomfortably in their pews.
Already pressed for time,
they calculate how much more of a donation
will exempt them from committee work.

A few busy people sit at attention to receive
their new assignments.
They gravitate toward the center of activity
and of influence wherever they go.

Some slip away unnoticed after the sermon,
their minds in upheaval like birds in flight,
having long sought work to do according to their purpose
but no one has offered it to them.

DARK MOTHER

Sometimes during the
celebration of Holy Mass
all the light-filled actions
of priest and servers
would seem to flatten out,
as if printed on a sheet of parchment

And just behind them
– she sensed –
roiled an accursed entourage.
Gibbering, whirling in their myriads,
scheming against the innocent.

In these moments,
she felt that she had only
to reach down
and her wrist would be clutched
in the iron grip of the Dark Mother
seeking to engage the enemy once more.

She wondered with apprehension
why she should be a nexus
between the worlds.
Then she thought,
We all are.

O ANTIPHONS

Another student hinted
that here was something special,
something worth hearing.
So we stayed downtown after dark,
bundled against December winds,
and climbed endless marble steps

up the Capitoline hill
picking our way through
hulking colossi, heroic statues
in the Forum, some grotesquely
dismembered, a head fallen here,
there a huge hand cradling a kitten.

Finally, oaken doors open onto
an oasis of light, and golden mosaic.
A mellifluous choir alternates verses
of the evensong of Vespers
in this, the Virgin's Altar of Heaven.

A gaunt cleric mounts to the lectern.
With purpose (who knows – perhaps
this is his only task all year) he intones
a fall of notes as clear as bells,
complex as raindrops into a pond:

O Wisdom, proceeding from the mouth of the Most High…
come and guide us in the ways of prudence.

Yet more marvellous
the crowd answers him back
without haste, without error,
from thousand-year old memory
of a sound as intricate as manuscript:

O Radiant Dawn, splendor of eternal light…
come and enlighten those who sit in darkness.

Night after night, the voices call to one another
in a crescendo of longing and expectation
that soothes as it inspires;
tracing itself on the mind of history,
fading not until it achieves its end.

O Ruler of Nations, and their heart's desire…
come and save us, whom you formed out of dust.

WATER CREATURES

Tufted Roman geese,
of a proud, ancient breed
sacred to Juno,
strut along the Tiber's banks.
Muskrat-like nutria
build their marshy nests
under the vacant eyes of marble statues
in Villa Doria Pamfili.
A scrappy grey tabby
filches minnows
from the flamingo pond
at the Pincio zoo in Villa Borghese.
All creatures considered common
and more or less filthy
busily pull things up from the depths
(surely none of us would want to
peer too far underneath the surface
of the Tiber – convenient disposal
system for all manner of thing,
since Rome's founding).
Yet they delight with their vitality,
moving amidst the ruins.
There was a time
when we were able
to go deeper, and not worry
about besmirching ourselves with mud.

CHRIST-BEARER

Did you never meet a
good priest, after all your time
in Rome? Of course. And
what was he like, the good priest?
He looked with compassion
at who spoke, no matter how busy;
had an inner lightness of being,
diffusing and charging all around.
The things I hate, he hated more;
and he laughed like a child of God.

EUCHARISTIC ADORATION

Sink down to the point at the center of the self
at the center of the universe.
White host in jeweled monstrance:
golden mandala reaching every place and time,
folding all contraries back within yourself
where no words are necessary
nor thought, but only a glance,
and we are suspended in joy like amber:
a solemn joy not very far from sorrow.
The old woman in front hisses her prayers.
Worship music leaks from a teen's earbuds.
We are earthen vessels to one another.

BEHAVIORAL HOSPITAL

Smells of pot roast and cabbage
down the halls from the cafeteria.
Heavy doors that open with a key.

Patients amble around the day room
muttering softly to others not seen
or looking in vain for anything sharp.

Nurses walk briskly by on errands
social workers conduct efficient groups
then disappear behind paperwork mountains.

How can they all be in such a hurry
in a place where so little ever happens?
Like leaves blown around the base of trees.

It is a place between our several worlds
where refuge can be sought for a time
from unbearable strain in living.

Yet even here, should anyone give vent
to anguish, striking out, they are managed
as quickly and efficiently as possible.

Thus it becomes subversion, revolution,
to cross over and visit Christ who is sick
and not count it as a billable hour.

LOST FRIEND

As I walked down the sidewalk
a calico sitting in a front yard
(I thought she was tame)
took fright at the sight of me
and ran into the street where cars rush by.

So with a friend who is lost
the ties of trust withdrawn
leaving a dizzying void
as I reel back from her shocked reaction
to words that – too late – reveal a double meaning.

How is it possible to endure
with that last scene reverberating ever?
Even were it possible to add, or unsay,
what then? As a crashing, hulking thing
I am become, so she will not view me otherwise.

Yet I can try. For the most subtle Spirit of all
bears the gross projections we place on to it.
As am I without my friend, so is Christ without us.
Not only in vigils of hermits, but in bumbling vicissitudes
of friends, his Passion comes to full measure.

HOPE

Walking by the side of the road
in the cold rain
the small creature forges ahead
undeterred by the loud, dark shapes
splashing past.
She neither knows nor wonders
how she got to this narrow strip,
only believes firmly
that it must be crossed
for the sake of the new life inside her
one paw in front of the other.

After a time,
one of the dark shapes stops.
A door opens,
compassionate arms reach out
to take her inside
out of the wet
further up the road
to where lights shine
in the windows of houses.

LEONIE MARTIN

Kind old nun, gracing the cloister halls like a sunbeam
encouraging the young ones with a kind word or joke
surprising the sick with a heating pad in winter.

She says, "what a mercy I am here!" And they wonder
as they catch her faraway gaze in unguarded reminiscence
or those sleeping by hear her cry out at night.

As she is pulled back into the inarticulate rage of her frail body
her worried mother praying that she might develop self-control
the pious sisters joking about the black sheep, the cuckoo.

And she hears again the voice of her tormenter – the practical one
amidst all the piety – someone must teach the child to obey. Speak
(supposing she could) and I will hurt you. That one mercifully went away.

She dresses, and muses: the younger ones don't recall the strict old days.
Twice they hedged her about with rules, and let her go home in defeat
her noble gift of self thrown back in her teeth, before she got to stay.

And in the day, she smiles and is glad, and says, "What a mercy
I am here," where the Omega is the Alpha: Love saw her aright
and so she spends her days devising acts of love anew.

POOR MAN, RICH MAN

I fear you, for I cannot tell
what you will do or say.
Rudderless, I beg at your gate
without assurance of entry.

Not even possessed
of myself, I change my rags
according to circumstance –
what has gained favor for others.

Then once I have your ear,
I am become like a courtier,
indulging in rich portions
of your time and attention.

But all this discourse about
my few meager possessions –
though for a while may hold you –
will find me back outside the gate.

Would that I could sit for a time
in peace with my own poor man.
Then I could meet you, brother,
and not seek to be filled by you.

STEALING AWAY

Dishes with scraps of lasagna,
cream cake.
Glasses with dregs of ruby wine
after the feast-day meal
(always the same feast).
Relatives gathered around
soft murmur, flickering light
of the television set.
Yet there is someone
who still feels hunger, thirst
for the Living Word
after all the conversation and eating.
But to walk out, in the middle
of a program? St. Jane Frances
stepped over her grown son
who lay down in the doorway
on her way to the convent.
This is nothing compared to that.
Is she upset? They will wonder.
So they will wonder.
Is she sick? Yes, "revive me
with raisin cakes, for I am
sick with love."

AGNES OF MONTEPULCIANO

Yes, we chose her to lead us,
on a time, when we all were young.
She spoke of heaven honey-sweet;
and taught us gently.

Well, once elected, she spoke to us no more
– complained the wizened old women.
The priests were here to make her a saint.
Well, even so.

She holed herself up in her little room
sleeping on the earthen floor.
If we went in to see her, ever so quietly,
she yelled at us

that we disturbed her prayer to Baby Jesus
and his Mother Mary.
We were so poor, we just wanted to say
we had no bread or oil.

Although when we had looked again,
the larder did seem to be full…
Not that she cared about eating –
skinny little thing.

HEDDLES

Whence come these cords,
invisible rules that circumscribe
every day of life, ever more?
Beyond reason, beyond
what any code requires:
down to articles of dress,
and which route to walk.
He rails against them, and yet
to choose differently lands him
in sticky situations.
Thus dejected, shall he ask
pardon for his wilfulness?
But pardon from whom?
What deity issues such
dictator-demands?
And after all it seems that the
rules are not there to oppress,
but rather to guide him into
alignment with all that is,
from which flows strength
and fortunate coincidence.
What then of those who
run lightly through the world,
forging their own path?
Theirs perhaps is the gift of
embroidery; but his other way,
bound up with the warp
and woof of the cloth itself.

SACRED HEART

Bleeding rose-red image
thorns over pleading eyes.
Burden of melancholy
in remembrance

as of a traveler
whose train arrives too late
and to whom the bereaved
grimly serve tea.

Martha's hands thrown up
at his perceived demands
and clumsy companions.
"They will hardly feed themselves."

But he is the molten core, restoring
the very self after four days;
sitting not awaiting service,
he who once came too late.

ARM'S LENGTH

Having at one time
become fascinated
by what was not you
but rather the trappings and rubrics
with which we surround you

I find I must ever after
hold you, the Beloved,
at arm's length
and think of you without thinking of you
which is most painful.

Not through any fault
or defect of yours
but because of the bent
of my mind, spinning concentric orbits
down around your luster.

Much better for me
to start from the earth.
Sweep the floor,
cook the meal, sit with those who visit
as if sitting with you.

THE LAST DAY

One day, long ago,
a road ran through trees
just kissed with autumn;
and in the champagne sky,
streaked with pink and blue,
rose the smell of smoked
meats from the butcher.
Trembling on the edge
of melancholy,
poised forever on the
moment before ending.
A day among ordinary folk
buying paper-wrapped meats
from a country farmer
is like – in its loss – to the
endings of all kingdoms
and principalities.
No greater beauty crumbles,
nor symmetry is marred,
when the Taj Mahal or
Florentine David falls
as after that smoky sunset.
Write down your legacy.
Fold up the paper.
Cast it into the fire,
so the fragrance of it
will waft through the ages.

AGING PRAYER

Now that I am old
it occurs to me
to smile indulgently at the Christ –
big strapping man striding
all about the countryside –
as the feeble are wont to
shake their heads at the young
as if to ask: what can you know
of illness, beyond a runny nose,
a rash, a fever whose course
was measured by days spent indoors?
You suffered for a day –
you who did not live to grow old –
and so won for yourself a hero's glory.
But what can you know of
slow decrepitude
or the scythe that cuts down in middle age,
or the pain that is nursed from youth on?
Complaining still, my thought discerns
threads of gray in his hair
that were not there before.
Jaw no longer so squarely set,
hue of skin multiplied into all shades
all ages and conditions.
And with indulgent smile, he replies,
"I learned of it through you, dear."

GLIMPSING NEW MEXICO

Red dust, dogs barking,
flatlands running up to forested mountains.
Roadrunner, flowering cactus,
prune-and-apple pie;
adobe houses in every rose-hue of clay.

A mighty sorrow, too:
time like a dark pool of tears,
welling up, flowing in all directions,
worrying at the stones of history
as if to find a past different than it was.

Visitors from the big cities,
accustomed to forward motion, offer
encouragement; but we have little
practice in sitting broken-hearted vigil
for a god who does not dwell in a structure.

For it seemed, in that place,
that God strides tall as the sky
and the Virgin dons all the colors of the seasons.
A Spirit-wind blows all the time,
and the Light of the World plays with shadow.

CAT

Silent, alternately loving and absent, on his own terms.
Soft, accepting care, briefly fierce with flash of teeth or claw.
Pleasure-loving, moving through life with utter self-assurance;
my own spirit animal and guide, my unwitting patron saint.

ACKNOWLEDGMENTS

The inner work that went into preparation for this volume could not have been accomplished without the teaching and friendship of many people who have been associated in one way or another with The Jung Center, Houston, TX. The Desert Rain intentional community of Chaparral, NM provided a vital link with the centering prayer of Thomas Keating, O.C.S.O.

Many selfless and dedicated Dominican and Carmelite fathers welcomed me at their respective universities in Rome half a lifetime ago. I remember especially Michael Tavuzzi, O.P. and Reginald Foster, O.C.D., whose brilliant eccentricity jolted many a young cleric into the World of Ideas.

This book could not have reached its present form without the insightful encouragement of developmental editor, Max Regan, as well as the generous and soulful reflections offered by Poet Carol Guerrero-Murphy.

Finally, I would like to thank my husband, Jeremy Clark, for his support in reading several drafts and generally putting up with my absence during the writing; my sister Teresa – a published author in her own right – for her unfailing encouragement; my brother Tom, for unexpected laughter; and my parents, Maria and Sal, for raising us up among the flowers, with love.

NOTES

SCRUPULOSITY
An OCD-type condition characterized by religious themes such as extreme anxiety over having committed or failed to atone for relatively small sins.

GOSSIP
As membership in traditional religious orders wanes, some sisters and brothers have converted the use of their larger properties to hospitality. Thus, the setting is a pensione or boarding-house for students, run by nuns – common in Rome.

PARABLE OF THE TALENTS
Title refers to Matthew 25:15, "To one he gave five talents, to another two, to another one, to each according to his ability" (New Revised Standard Version).

O ANTIPHONS
From at least the eighth century in the Roman liturgy, these verses have traditionally introduced the Canticle of Mary at Vespers on the last seven days of Advent. Each one begins with an O followed by an attribute of Christ drawn from Old Testament prophecy: Root of Jesse, Key of David, etc.

EUCHARISTIC ADORATION
A practice of quiet prayer during which the consecrated wafer from Mass – believed to contain the real presence of Jesus – is displayed in a special holder called a monstrance.

LEONIE MARTIN
A lesser-known older sister of St. Thérèse of Lisieux, the Little Flower, whose image is found in Catholic churches worldwide. Léonie (1863-1941) had early behaviors consistent with developmental challenges, for which no treatment was available beyond faith, but which stood in the way of her dream of becoming a nun. The Visitation cloister finally offered her reasonable accommodations.

POOR MAN, RICH MAN
An initial, non-exhaustive approach to the use of poverty here is to consider the DSM-5 language of social deficits.

STEALING AWAY
The scriptural reference is to the Song of Solomon 2:5.

AGNES OF MONTEPULCIANO
A Dominican nun known for the power of her prayer. Although difficult to tell at such a distance (she died in 1317), I believe her biography shows some autism spectrum traits, such as the communication difficulties highlighted here.

This poem imaginatively recreates an episode when a priest gathering evidence for Agnes' canonization (i.e. official declaration as a saint) interviewed elderly nuns who knew her as girls.

HEDDLES

Heddles are part of a loom, made of cord or wire. Each warp thread passes through the eye of a heddle, which holds it for the passage of the weft threads during weaving. I am indebted to Carol Guerrero-Murphy for the suggestion of this imagery.

AGING PRAYER

The scriptural context is Colossians 1:24, "In my flesh I am completing what is lacking in Christ's afflictions."

GLIMPSING NEW MEXICO

An adobe house is constructed from sun-dried bricks of earth and straw, with timbers (vigas) supporting the roof. Some of the oldest continuously inhabited examples of these are in the Taos Pueblo, NM, where the people carry the memory of the violent as well as deeply spiritual history of this area. In the Pueblo church, a statue of the Virgin Mary is clothed in a different color four times a year, to symbolize her close identification with Mother Earth.

ABOUT THE AUTHOR

Andrea's journey as a writer spans the academic, financial, and behavioral health sectors. She earned a doctorate in Philosophy from the University of St. Thomas (Houston) in 2008 and has taught philosophy as an adjunct instructor. Concurrently, she also had a career in the mortgage banking industry. Changing careers in 2010, she earned her MS in Psychology from OLLU-Houston. She lived in Rome, Italy for several years. She has worked in both inpatient and outpatient hospitalization settings, in addition to her private practice. All these experiences afford her a unique perspective.

Contact the author at: https://www.andreamessineolpc.com/

Typefaces Used:

TYPEFACE: PERPETUA TITLING MT – LIGHT
TYPEFACE: GARAMOND – Garamond